Short Cycle Rides

Around

Wells

&

Glastonbury

John Plaxton

with illustrations by Jill Plaxton

For Mum and Dad

First Edition April 1994
ISBN 0 9520669 1 2

Cycleway Books
2 Cork Terrace
Bath BA1 3BE

© **John Plaxton 1994**

Design and Typesetting by Cycleway Books
Printed in Great Britain by The University of the West of England Printing and Stationery Services

All rights reserved. No part of this publication may be reproduced, stored in a retrieval system or transmitted, in any form or by any means, electronic, mechanical, photocopying, recording or otherwise, without prior permission from the copyright holder.

Whilst every care has been taken in the preparation of this guide, neither the author nor publisher will be responsible for any loss, damage or inconvenience caused by inaccuracies.

Contents

Introduction 1
Some Cycling Tips 2
Local Cycle Shops 4
Cycle Hire 4
Local Tourist Information Centres 5
Using The Routes 5
Street Maps - Wells & Glastonbury 7

Ten Cycle Routes   Distance (miles) Grade   Page

1. Wells - Bleadney - Easton - Wookey Hole - Wells 11 ½   Easy   11

2. Glastonbury - Baltonsborough - Barton St David - Butleigh - Street - Glastonbury   16 ½   Moderate   16

3. Glastonbury - Godney - Coxley - West Pennard - Kennard Moor - Glastonbury   20   Easy   21

4. Glastonbury - Godney - Westhay - Burtle - Catcott - Shapwick - Glastonbury   22   Easy   27

5. Wells - Wookey Hole - Priddy - Cheddar - Wedmore - Mudgley - Wells   23   Strenuous   31

6. Wells - East Horrington - Binegar - Stratton-on-the-Fosse - Holcombe - Shepton Mallet - Wells   24   Strenuous   37

7. Wells - Dulcote - North Wootton - Pilton - East Pennard - Baltonsborough - Glastonbury - Wells   27   Moderate   43

8. Glastonbury - West Bradley - Ditcheat - Castle Cary - Baltonsborough - Glastonbury   29   Moderate   48

9. Glastonbury - Charlton Mackrell - Somerton - Langport - High Ham - Glastonbury   30   Moderate   53

10. Wells - Priddy - Blagdon - Chew Stoke - East Harptree - Bishop Sutton - Wells   32 or 21   Strenuous   59

Index 66

Sir Samuel Hood Monument, Butleigh Wood

Introduction

Let's be honest, I'm a lazy cyclist. For some people, their idea of a great day out is a 50 mile ride along roaringly busy roads or a lung-busting pedal up a series of massive hills, often along tracks that are so rough that letting your eyes wander from the front wheel could result in immediate disaster. This is not for me or, I suspect, the majority of weekend cyclists.

This book is all about relaxing cycle rides in the local countryside, on quiet lanes where cars are few and far between. I go slowly enough to be able to look at the scenery and wildlife along the way, visiting places of interest, pubs and tea shops, not getting too hot or tired in the process. And what a brilliant locality it is for doing just that.

Now, as you set off on your bike with this book, you can enjoy circular rides starting from the historic City of Wells or the mystical centre of Glastonbury. You can pedal into the Mendip Hills and the Chew Valley beyond, explore the refreshingly flat Somerset Levels, or visit the apple orchards on the way to small towns like Langport and Somerton. The routes are designed so that they follow the quietest possible roads. Some of the routes even have short off-road sections for the mountain bikers. I usually try to avoid the worst of the hills although, if this is a problem for you, I would avoid the Mendips. I never cease to be fascinated by the wildlife that surrounds me when I am out on my bike and I have mentioned birds, insects and plants that you may see at different times of the year.

If your bike has sat in the shed for years accumulating dust, and the children are hassling you to go on rides with them, or you just want to explore this beautiful area in a relaxed way then this is the book for you. Pick a nice day for your ride, take it slowly and happy pedalling.

John Plaxton

Some Cycling Tips

1. Before setting out check over your bike and make sure it is in good working order.
2. There are several rides which include very steep sections. Check your brakes before the descents. Gears would be an advantage on some of the more hilly rides.
3. Try not to ride an unbalanced bike. Carry luggage sensibly, either in panniers or a rucksack. If you use a basket or elastic grips, make sure items cannot come loose and fall off. It is advisable to have close fitting clothes and shoe laces securely fastened so that there is no chance of them getting caught in the chain or wheels.
4. Carry a small tool kit, including a puncture repair kit. If you bring a spare inner-tube remember you may need a spanner to remove the wheel before you can fit it!
5. A First Aid kit is a good idea as is some form of identification in case of an accident.
6. If you are cycling during the day, bright or fluorescent clothing is sensible; so are reflective strips at night. It is compulsory to use front and rear lights and also to have a red reflector to the rear of your bike after dark.
7. Ride in single file if roads are busy or narrow. Never ride more than two abreast.
8. Bear in mind that your brakes will not work so well in the wet. Go slower, and leave more room between yourself and other cyclists.
9. I have tried to warn of the busiest and most dangerous stretches of road in my route guides, but please be careful all the time during your rides. Be prepared to get off and walk your bike at certain places if you are uncertain about traffic.

10. Always be aware of the Highway Code. Do not give other cyclists a bad name by ignoring the rules.
11. The wearing of a cycle helmet is advisable, and may reduce the risk of serious head injury.
12. The use of a bell is a polite way of announcing your presence, especially when approaching pedestrians. They may not have seen or heard you coming. A word of thanks after someone has stood aside for you is always appreciated.
13. Lock up your cycle every time you leave it, even if you are only going inside a shop for a minute. If it's a valuable bike don't let it out of your sight even if it is locked up. Parts can be removed by thieves in seconds.
14. Unruly dogs can be a nuisance to cyclists. If one comes at you try to keep quiet and continue on slowly. Try not to catch their eye. You may want to speed up but, from personal experience, I have found that this can make them more inclined to snap at your ankles.
15. At certain times of year, after the hedges have been cut, try to avoid clippings at the sides of the road. If not, you are highly likely to get punctures from the thorns.

Local Cycle Shops

Bikes 'n' Bits
49 St Cuthberts St Wells (0749) 670260

City Cycles
80 High Street Wells (0749) 675096

Franks Cycles
North St Langport (0458) 250348

Pedalers
8 Magdalene St Glastonbury (0458) 831117

Street Bikes
157 High St Street (0458) 47882

TJ Cycles
42 Westend Street (0458) 841715

Cycle Hire

City Cycles
80 High Street Wells (0749) 675096

Pedalers
8 Magdalene St Glastonbury (0458) 831117

Local Tourist Information Centres

Taunton
Taunton Library, Corporation St
Tel. (0823) 274785

Bridgwater (only open during the summer)
High St
Tel. (0278) 427652

Glastonbury
1 Marchants Bldgs, Northload St
Tel. (0458) 832954

Wells
Town Hall, Market Pl.
Tel. (0749) 672552

Cheddar (only open during the summer)
The Gorge
Tel. (0934) 744071

Using the Routes

Distances

The route guides state roughly how long the rides are in miles. Each ride starts and finishes from the same, easy-to-find location. Because all the rides are circular you can start and finish them anywhere along the way. Without stops a slow cyclist may expect to do about 6-7 miles in an hour, depending on the terrain. If you are new to cycling why not start with a short ride. You could be surprised by how quickly you cover the distance.

Grading

The grade of each ride gives you an idea of the number, length and severity of hills along the way. Bear in mind that the direction and strength of the wind can make quite a difference to how easy you find the ride. If it is windy try to find a ride that starts into the wind, while you still have plenty of energy.

Easy: Just a few hills which are short and not too steep.

Moderate: One or two hills but you should not have to get off and push if your bike has gears.

Strenuous: Be prepared to get off and push unless you have lots of gears and are very fit. There may also be some steep downhill sections.

Maps

I would strongly recommend that you use the maps as suggested in the route guides. The plans that appear in this book are for reference only and are not necessarily accurate or to scale.

O.S. 1:50,000 Landranger 182, Weston-Super-Mare and Bridgwater area.

O.S. 1:50,000 Landranger 183, Yeovil and Frome.

O.S. 1:50,000 Landranger 193, Taunton and Lyme Regis.

Countryside Code

I hope that you use these routes as an excuse to get out into the countryside around this beautiful area of Somerset. However, if you do not wish to offend other walkers and cyclists and those who live and work in the countryside, please leave things as you find them.

Starting and Finishing Your Cycle Rides

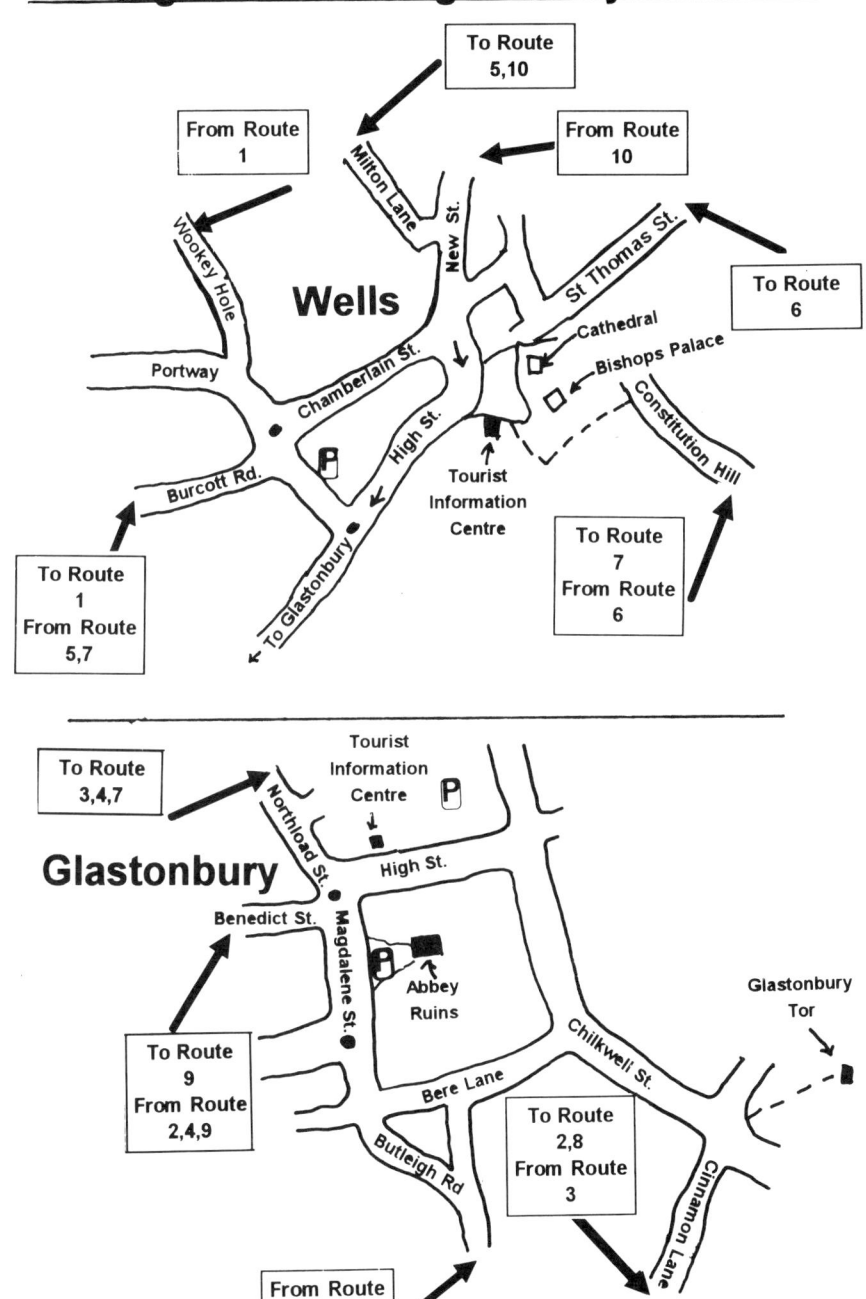

Ten
Cycle Rides
Around
Wells and Glastonbury

Wells Catherdral

Outline to Route 1

Wells - Bleadney - Easton - Wookey Hole - Wells

Distance: 11 ½ miles

Grade: Easy

Maps: O.S. 1:50,000 Landranger 182 or 183

Summary : This ride is very short and reasonably flat so it could be suitable for young children as long as you do not pick a day and time when there is likely to be heavy tourist traffic on the road between Wookey Hole and Wells. If you are out with children why not get them into the habit of looking behind before they start and stop, before signalling and making manoeuvres on the road. This could give them a head start in preparing for their Cycling Proficiency Tests.

The ride begins with a pedal along the lanes that run between the Somerset Levels and the Mendip Hills. In a mile or two you may notice a raised mound on your left. This was the site of Fenny Castle. There is little to see now although you cannot miss the Inn with the same name.

Continuing on, you will cross the B3139 and find yourself on one of the quietest roads around Wells. It is very narrow and at times muddy; almost like a farm track. From near here you can make a detour to one of the longest fords in the country - a good way to cool yourself down if it is a hot summer's day, although you should not forget that cars occasionally use this road too! Ahead of you, the Mendip Hills rise up 250 metres. Don't worry though, on this ride you will only have to cycle a short distance uphill before the descent into Wookey Hole. By the way, you can also make a detour to Ebbor Gorge on the way to Wookey Hole. This is a mini version of Cheddar Gorge but much less spoilt. You can enjoy an interesting walk through some beautiful woodland. At the top car park there are information plaques telling you how the gorge was formed and what to look out for in the way of plant and animal life.

Once at Wookey Hole you could be glad that you only did a short ride. It can take quite a time to see all the sights. The village itself is a pleasant place to walk around. The name comes from the Celtic "Wocig", meaning an animal trap. There is evidence that early cave dwellers set up large traps using the caves. Large piles of animal bones have been found. In addition to the caves the village grew up around a paper-mill that was built in 1610 near where the River Axe emerges from the mountain side. The mill suffered a devastating fire and was rebuilt by the Hodgkinson family in 1855. They also built housing for the workers, the church and village hall. It was not until the 1920's that they decided to exploit the tourism potential of the caves at Wookey. Nowadays it is billed as Somerset's No.1 visitors' attraction. In the summer it is open 9.30am-5.30pm, during the winter 10.30am-4.30pm, Tel. (0749) 672243. After the tour of the caves you can visit the paper-mill, a hall of mirrors, and an Edwardian Fair. There also is a restaurant for snacks.

From Wookey Hole there is an undulating stretch of road that takes you back to Wells.

Route 1

1. The ride starts from the centre of Wells. Leave the city on Burcott Road (see map on page 7).
2. Continue straight along this road for about 3 miles. You will eventually come to a T-junction by Pine Tree Farm. Turn left and pedal past the Fenny Castle Country Inn.
3. In a while you will see a turning on the right, signposted Bleadney 1. Go down this road and you will come out at a T-junction with the B3139 road. Turn left, and then after about 200 metres right. You should see a sign saying Bleadney on the corner here.

Wells

4. A little further along, you can make an entertaining detour to one of the longest fords in England at around 100 metres; it's sort of half river, half road. A mile beyond Bleadney take the second road on the right, just before a small stone bridge. Now take the next road on the left. You will soon come to the ford. Do not pedal through it unless water levels are very low. There are lots of slippery rocks hidden beneath the water.

   To return to our route, cycle back to the small stone bridge mentioned above. Cross the bridge and follow this quiet stretch of road until you come to Easton, at a crossroads with the A371 road.

5. Go straight ahead at the crossroads and pedal up a hill to a T-junction. Now turn left and continue uphill. Take it slowly; this is only a short ride so there is no need to overdo it. At the top of the hill turn left if you want to visit Ebbor Gorge. You will soon see it on your right. If not, then turn right and freewheel down the hill into Wookey Hole.

6. From Wookey Hole, the route follows the Wells road all the way back to the city centre. *At certain times of day this road can get quite busy with people visiting and returning from the caves. Be cautious, wear something bright and cycle in single file.*

Route 1

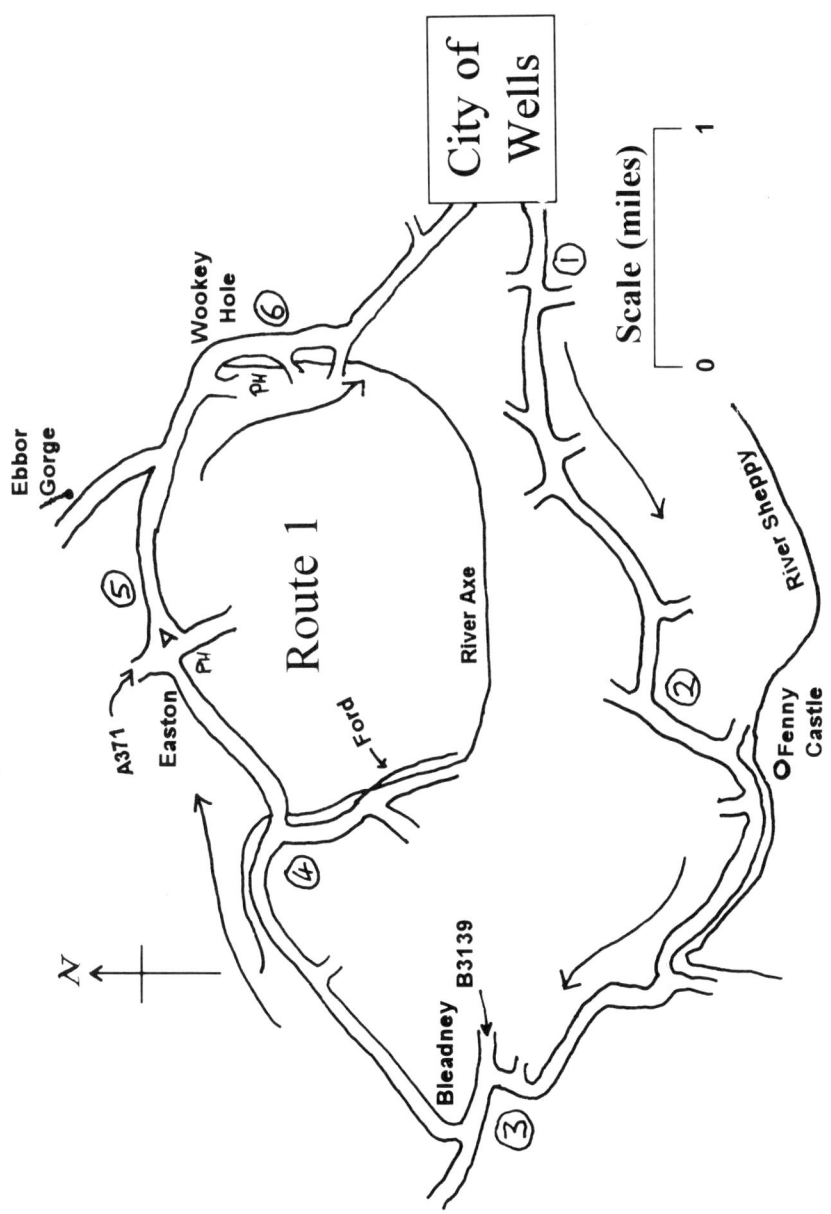

Outline to Route 2

Glastonbury - Baltonsborough - Barton St David - Butleigh - Compton Dundon - Street - Glastonbury

Distance: 16 ½ miles (optional 1 mile "off road")

Grade: Moderate

Map: O.S. 1:50,000 Landranger 182

Summary : This is one of my favourite rides in this book. It takes you along roads that are often deserted, and through some pretty villages. It also has a short stretch of off-road cycling that will tax even the experienced, if there has been a lot of rain.

At the start of this ride there are two places you may wish to visit even before you have left Glastonbury. Firstly, as you pass through the outskirts of town look out for the Rural Life Museum on your right. It's a 14th century Abbey Barn with lots of old farm implements, ducks and chickens around it. Inside you will get a good picture of what farming life must have been like 150 years ago. It is open all year round, but summer opening times during the week are 10.00am-5.00pm, and 2.00pm-6.00pm at weekends Tel. (0458) 831197. Secondly, a little further along on your left you can see the Chalice Well. This used to be a water supply for the town. Information plaques tell of the many legends surrounding the well.

Once out of Glastonbury it is a pleasant pedal across Kennard Moor to the village of Baltonsborough. It is hard to believe that this whole area was heavily wooded a thousand years ago. Most of the forests disappeared as

firewood for the Abbey at Glastonbury. I first did this ride in the autumn as the leaves were falling, and with the trees heavy with apples. The fruit trees prefer to grow on these "upland" areas, so they often surround the island villages. Many of the cider orchards are clearly very old. The trees are twisted and broken with age but still covered in apples in a good year. Thankfully, there seem to be a few newly-planted apple orchards in this area with their ordered lines of trees all of uniform height. In the 17th century every man, woman and child drank the equivalent of a quart of cider a day. The wages were made up in part by cider - The Cider Truck. It was used as a stimulant due to the poor cereal diet. Drink must have helped the agricultural peasants get through the day. Although it was known as the poor man's drink, there was little alternative because well and river water was frequently undrinkable.

The route now continues on to Barton St David and Butleigh. These villages now seem popular with commuters. There hardly seems a stone or roofing tile out of place in the older properties and there are many newer houses surrounding the old centres of the villages. For all this they are agreeable places to pedal through.

Beyond Butleigh there is a short climb up through the

woods. You may see Buzzards at any time of the year when cycling in this area. These large birds of prey feed on rabbits, birds, insects and carrion. They like to soar over areas of woodland whilst making their plaintive mewing call. You can occasionally see them trying to hover, but they lack the skill and finesse of the Kestrel. It is common to see Buzzards being mobbed by rooks. Birds of prey are understandably very unpopular with other animal life.

If you decide not to cycle off-road through the woods, you could visit the monument to Sir Samuel Hood for a picnic. Born locally, he became a naval hero during the late 18th century. As long as the graffiti does not get any worse, you should be able to read more about Sir Samuel from the inscription on the monument.

The ride now continues on to Street. This town is famous for the Clarks shoe factory. Indeed the Quaker founders almost created the whole place including shops, schools and churches. You can visit the Shoe Museum during the summer months. Entrance is free, with opening times Mon.-Fri. 10.00am-4.45pm and Sat. 10.00am-4.30pm.

From Street there is a cycle route that takes you back to Glastonbury so you can avoid the worst of the traffic.

Route 2

1. The route starts from the entrance to the Abbey ruins in the centre of Glastonbury. Using the map on page 7, pedal out of town on the A361 road, turning right down Cinnamon Lane. *Be careful of oncoming vehicles here.*
2. After about 200 metres take the next right turn. Now continue on this narrow road for about 3 miles. You will eventually come out at a T-junction. Go right here. Pedal through Baltonsborough, following the signs to Barton St David.

Route 2

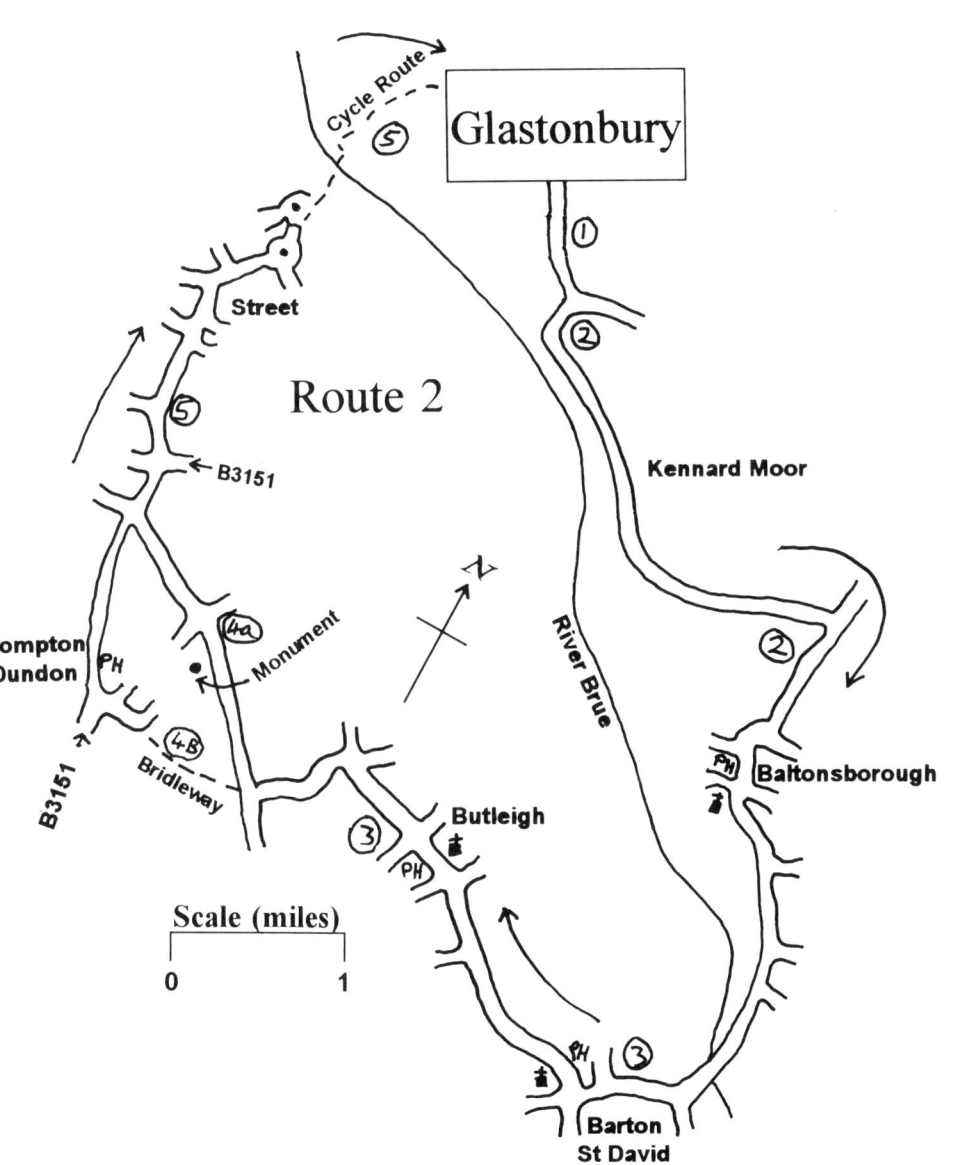

3. At the centre of Barton St David turn right at a crossroads and follow the signs to Butleigh. After a further 2 miles you will come to another crossroads with the Rose and Portcullis Inn on your left. Go straight ahead here.
4. Shortly you will come to a staggered crossroads. Turn left and pedal uphill past Butleigh Wood to a T-junction. You can now choose which way to go.
   a. **For non-mountain bikers** turn right here. You will eventually find yourself freewheeling down a long hill to a crossroads at the junction with the B3151 road (you can see the monument to Sir Samuel Hood half way down the hill on the left). Go right towards Street.
   b. **For experienced mountain bikers,** follow the signposted bridleway straight ahead at the T-junction. *This path is steep and can be very muddy, so be careful.* If you get lost try to follow a slightly wider path to the right going downhill all the time. This will lead you to a gate at the bottom of the hill. Go through the gate, and continue along the track until you return to metalled road again. You are now in Compton Dundon. Go right, then left until you reach the B3151 road. Now turn right, and climb a hill to a crossroads. keep going straight here. *This road can be quite busy.*
5. Fork left by a large blue sign for Street (ignore the turning to Higher Brooks). Follow this road towards the centre of Street. Keep going straight ahead at several crossroads until you come to the High Street. Turn right and cycle through the town centre to a roundabout beyond. Continue on the Glastonbury road. Just before you come to the next roundabout you will see a cycle path. This will lead you all the way back to the centre of Glastonbury.

Outline to Route 3

Glastonbury - Godney - Coxley - Queen's Sedge Moor - West Pennard - Coxbridge - Kennard Moor - Glastonbury

Distance: 20 miles

Grade: Easy

Maps: O.S. 1:50,000 Landranger 182 or 183

Summary : This could be a good ride for you if steep hills are a problem. The route mostly stays on the Somerset Levels and is therefore extremely flat. Make sure you do not pick a day that is too windy though, otherwise it can feel as if you are pedalling uphill half of the time. This ride would be good to take children on. The roads are so quiet that you are unlikely to see more than a handful of cars.

Starting from Glastonbury it is not long before you are onto the Somerset Levels on the way to Godney. This is a charming little hamlet. Have a look at the walls of some of the small cottages as you pedal along. Built on the soft peaty ground, many sag and bow alarmingly. This gives them a certain character but perhaps heartache to their owners. New properties on the Levels are built on concrete rafts with deep pile foundations beneath, which makes construction costs very high. Another problem with some of the older cottages on the Levels is the damp. It was said that you could watch the damp rising up the walls every year.

The levels have a large population of Grey Heron. You are almost certain to see them on your cycle rides. With the rhynes and rivers being so full of fish, eels and other items of food this is not surprising. Unfortunately, the Heron seem more shy of bicycles than cars and will often fly off as you go by. Their large size and bent neck makes them unmistakeable in flight. If you are out on the Levels during the early summer the roadside ditches may be filled with Yellow Flag Iris. These aptly named plants like damp places. Their large yellow flower heads are very conspicuous as you pedal along. You may also see the beautiful Marsh Marigolds or King Cups in flower in the ditches. Looking like huge Butter Cups, they are supposed to give protection from both witches and lightening!

Although most of this ride is on the flat, there is a short excursion onto the slightly raised land around West Pennard. A few old apple orchards are dotted about the village today but in the past there were so many fruit trees in this area that the blossom in spring was said to have been a tourist attraction. Cattle graze in the orchards until mid-August (until the Priddy Fair) and the fruit is harvested in late autumn. There are hundreds of varieties of apple trees, but for cider-making they are divided into sweets, bittersweets, bittersharps, and sharps. Nowadays, commercial makers use about 75% bittersweets and a few sharps, due to the drinker's taste for sweet and strong ciders. You may see signs for local farmhouse cider on sale as you pedal along. Give it a try, but don't risk being arrested for being drunk in charge of a bicycle. You will find it very different from the clear, commercial drink. Some say it's an acquired taste!

The ride finishes off with a pedal across Kennard Moor towards Glastonbury. This stretch of road is amazingly quiet and very good for cycling along. You are almost more likely to meet a herd of cattle on their way to be milked than a car.

Yellow Flag Irises

Route 3

1. The ride starts from the centre of Glastonbury. Leave town on the B3151 for Wedmore (see map on page 7). After about ½ a mile, just a beyond a bridge, turn right. Now continue on to the crossroads at the centre of Godney. Go straight ahead here.
2. At the next crossroads turn right following the sign to Fenny Castle. When you have passed the Fenny Castle

Country Inn turn right by Pine Tree Farm. Now pedal on for another 300 metres before turning right again. Watch out, this is an easy one to miss.

3. Soon you will come to a T-junction at Coxley village. Go left here and then immediately right, into Mill Lane. Follow this winding road to the A39 where you go straight across. *Take care, this road can be busy at times.*

4. You will soon come to a T-junction where you go right. If you now take the next right turn you should find yourself freewheeling down to the straight and very flat roads of Queen's Sedge Moor. At the first T-junction go left, and at the second, go right. After about 3 miles, look out for a junction on the right opposite Redlake Farm. Turn right here and follow the signs to West Pennard.

5. In about a mile you will come to the A361 road where you go right. There is a footpath all the way along here, which you may prefer to push along if the main road is busy. Just beyond the Red Lion Inn turn left, following the sign "West Bradley 2".

6. Soon you will see a road on the right signed Glastonbury 3 ½ miles. Now you have 3 turns in quick succession. Go right, then left, then very shortly, right again. This road will take you across Kennard Moor. It is very narrow and so little used that it often has grass growing on it!

7. When it seems that you have almost arrived at the foot of Glastonbury Tor you will come to a T-junction. Turn left. It is now quite a steep climb up the hill to the A361. Turn left to arrive back to the town centre.

Route 3

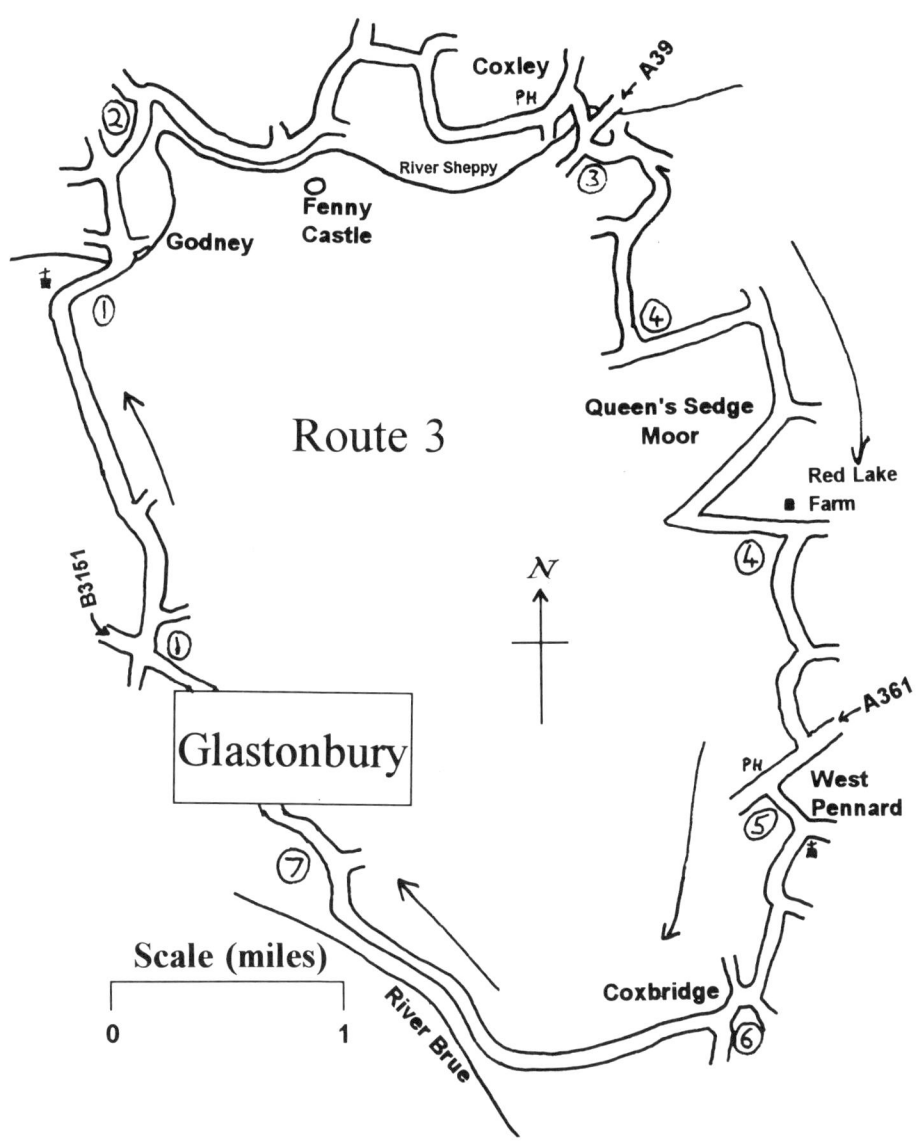

Peat Piles, Westhay Heath

Outline to Route 4

Glastonbury - Godney - Westhay - Burtle - Catcott - Shapwick - Ashcott - Glastonbury

Distance: 22 miles

Grade: Easy

Map: O.S. 1:50,000 Landranger 182

Summary: This ride takes you on an easy pedal through the Somerset Levels along narrow lanes where few cars venture and the wildlife is abundant.

Very soon after leaving Glastonbury you will find yourself pedalling along the mostly straight, narrow lanes through the Levels. At Godney have a look out for some large fish in the river on your left. Between here and Westhay you will be able to see peat workings, both past and present. The peat began to form about 3-4,000 years ago. You may notice that the piles of peat are different colours. Cotton Grass and other plants generated a light product whereas dark peat developed where the Sphagnum Moss grew most strongly. In the past most of the peat was burnt for fuel but today 95% is used for horticultural purposes. I hope that the delicate balance of flora and fauna of this area can be sustained with the increased mechanisation of the peat extraction. Huge mountains of peat waiting to be processed are an ugly site in such a beautiful landscape. With new alternatives now being developed, fewer gardeners should need to use this product in the future. One small benefit of this extraction is the new wildlife habitats which quickly develop in the waterlogged old peat beds. Reedmace, or

Bulrushes soon appear, ponds form and insect life thrives.

Westhay is known amongst archeologists as the location of the Sweet Track, the oldest trackway in the world. Discovered in the 1970's, it is believed to be 6,000 years old. Just beyond Westhay you could take a short detour to the Peat Moors Visitors Centre and find out more about the area. Open 10.00am-6.00pm during the summer, and closing a little earlier in the winter, the centre has an interesting display showing the history of the peat industry, archeology, and the flora and fauna of the area. You can also get snacks at the restaurant.

Approaching Catcott it is quite a surprise to be confronted by your first hill of the ride, up on to the Polden Hills. This village is full of flowers during the summer. Every garden is a riot of colour. The War Memorial certainly catches the eye. If you are thirsty, you will pass your last pub on this route as you enter Catcott. If not, the ride continues on through several villages founded on this higher ground, to the edge of the Levels.

After pedalling through Shapwick and Ashcott you will descend to the Levels again, passing more peat workings and some popular fishing lakes, created by the peat extraction. The ride finishes with a zig-zag route back to Glastonbury and the Tor.

Route 4

1. This route starts from Glastonbury, outside the car park to the Abbey ruins. Cycle up the High Street to the mini roundabout and take the B3151 road signposted to Wedmore and Meare (see the map on page 7).

2. In about ½ a mile, just after a bridge, take a right turn signposted to Godney. In about 2 miles you will come to

Route 4

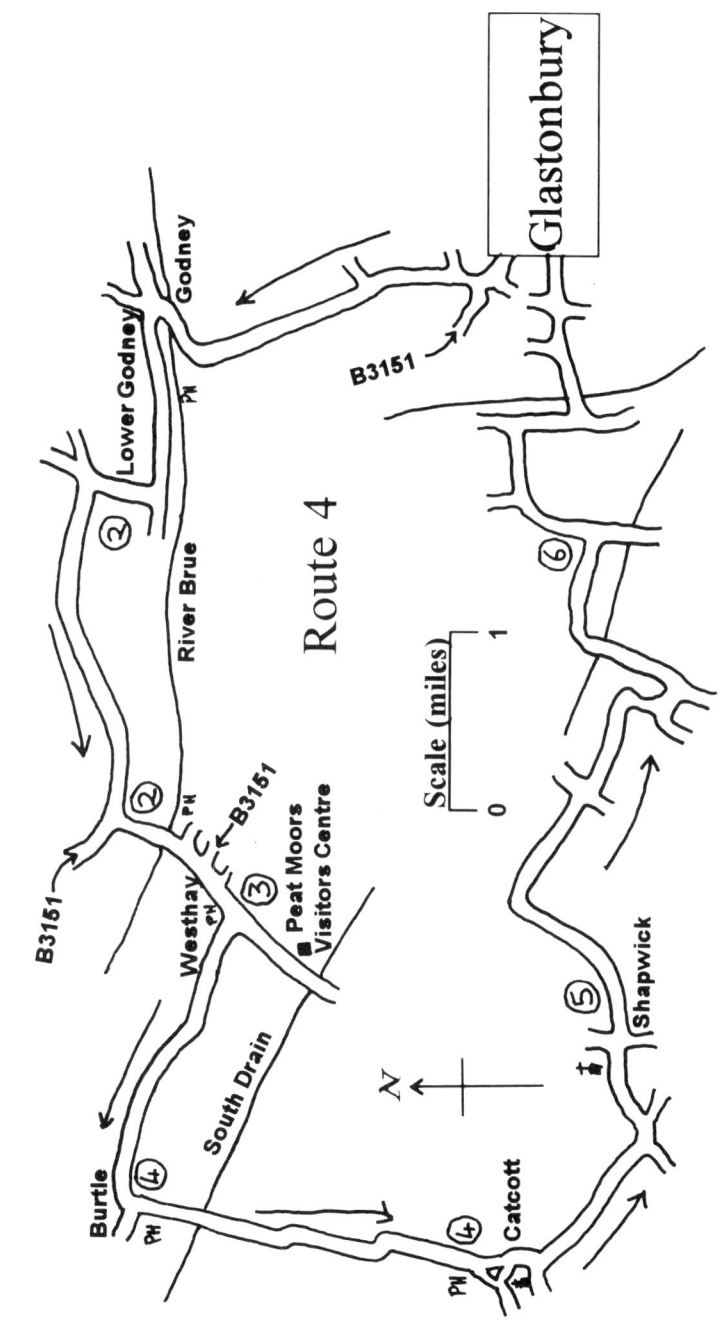

a crossroads. Go left and follow the signs firstly to Lower Godney and then on to Westhay. You will be going left at the B3151 road on the way.

3. At Westhay turn right off the main road, following the sign to Shapwick. Very shortly, take the next road on the right, signposted for Burtle. This turn is easy to miss.

   NB If you want to make a detour to the Peat Moors Visitors Centre ignore this last right turn for the moment. Carry straight on for another ½ mile. You will see it on your left, adjacent to a garden centre.

4. At Burtle go left by the Burtle Inn. You will come to Catcott in about 3 miles. This village seems a maze of different lanes. If you get lost follow the signs to Shapwick. When you enter Catcott, keep following the same road until you see the war memorial. Now go left, passing the village stores, and continue on to a T-junction with Lippetts Way. Turn left here and, after another mile, left again. You should now see the village sign for Shapwick.

5. At Shapwick go straight ahead at the crossroads. This next stretch of road seems little used. In 2 miles you will come to a staggered crossroads. Go left then right. Now, at the next 3 junctions go left. The last left turn is by Avalon Farm.

6. At the next T-junction you come to after Avalon Farm, go right and in about a ¼ mile turn left, pedalling over the River Brue. This road will lead you in an almost straight line back to the centre of Glastonbury.

Outline to Route 5

Wells - Wookey Hole - Priddy - Cheddar - Wedmore - Mudgley - Wells

Distance: 23 miles

Grade: Strenuous

Map: O.S. 1:50,000 Landranger 182

Summary: This ride has plenty to occupy both locals and visitors to the area. You can see one of the most famous gorges in the country, and tour some wonderful caves, as well as visit Mendip villages and the Somerset levels.

The route soon leaves the tortuous one-way system in Wells City Centre and climbs out past the Underwood Quarry on your left. Even from here there is a great view of Wells and the surrounding countryside. Now it is a short pedal to Wookey Hole. In the summer it is open 9.30am-5.30pm, during the winter 10.30am-4.30pm, tel. (0749) 672243. There is lots to see and it can get quite busy.

Get ready for quite a climb after Wookey Hole. If you need a rest on the way up why not visit the Ebbor Gorge nature trail. You can leave your bicycle at the car park, near the top of the hill.

By the time you get to Priddy you may need a rest. This is the highest village in Somerset! The famous sheep fair is held here annually, on the nearest Wednesday to 21st August. It was moved here from Wells in 1348 due to the "plague" in the city. The strange thatched structure on the village green is made up of stacks of hurdles which were used for the fair. Nowadays iron hurdles are used. There are

2 pubs to choose from, much frequented by hardy potholing enthusiasts. If you don't want to stop here you can very soon be in Cheddar; it is downhill almost all of the way.

The Cheddar Gorge was formed about 40,000 years ago. As the glaciers receded, after the last Ice Age, the melt-waters ate into the limestone rock thus forming the gorge and the vast network of caves and underground tunnels that you can see today. The town now seems to cater for a wide variety of tourists, which makes it look a little like a seaside resort at first glance, but there's still plenty to do here. The Tourist Information Centre is easy to find along the main road. The Cheddar Show Caves are open 10.00am-5.30pm in the summer, 10.30am-4.30pm in winter, tel. (0934) 742343. For a stunning view take a walk up Jacobs Ladder and visit Pavey's Lookout Tower. You could make an excursion to Axbridge or the local reservoir, along a short section of disused railway line made into a cyclepath.

From Cheddar it should be an easy pedal to Wedmore as long as the traffic is not too heavy. Wedmore is a pleasant place to visit, being much less touristy than Cheddar. It has a relaxed atmosphere. Now the route continues on to the Somerset Levels. The Willow trees are as much a part of the landscape of the Levels as the rhynes and rivers. They have a multitude of uses which have made them extremely important to local industry. Apart from containing enough tannin to tan leather, the bark also contains Acetyl-salicylic Acid, the basis of Aspirin. If you are cycling in this area during the autumn or winter you may see the Willows being pollarded. This is where the branches are cut off the trees and used for anything from thatching and fencing to firewood and basket-making. The best wood is even made into high quality artist's charcoal. Fewer willow trees seem to have that telltale pollarded stump these days. More of the trees are being allowed to grow to their full height. On the soft ground of the Levels this eventually means that the trunks will split, the lower branches will set roots, and the whole tree will become a tangled mass of branches along the road or river.

The ride finishes with a quiet pedal back to Wells. I can certainly recommend the Cloisters Café adjacent to the Cathedral. The tea and excellent cakes are just what you need after some tough pedalling.

Route 5

1. From the Tourist Information Office at the centre of Wells use the map on page 7 to get you started. Look out for and turn left into Mountery Road off the Bath Road. Shortly you will come to a crossroads. Go straight ahead into Milton Lane. You may have to push up this hill.

2. You will soon see a quarry on your left. Keep the fence on your left now. Soon the track becomes quite rough. Go left and follow the path down quite a steep hill. *Be extremely careful here, especially in wet weather*. At the end of the road go right, in front of Wayside Cottage, and continue on to Wookey Hole. You will see the large car park on your left at the centre of the village.

3. Continue up a hill through the village. The road flattens out for a time. Here take a right fork. It is now a long uphill pedal (or push in my case) past the Ebbor Gorge to Priddy.

4. From the centre of Priddy village follow the signs to Cheddar. Initially, the approach to Cheddar Gorge is a pleasantly gradual downhill, but towards the bottom it gets extremely steep and very winding. *Be very careful indeed. Road signs recommend that cyclists dismount for the last section, as you approach the town. You have been warned!*

5. Follow the road through the town until you come to a T-junction with the A371. Go right and follow the signs to Wedmore.

    NB You could make a detour to Axbridge a little further along, by following the blue signs for the cyclepath. The route starts from the back of an industrial estate off the road to the right, and takes you along a disused railway line skirting by the Cheddar Reservoir on your left.

Route 5

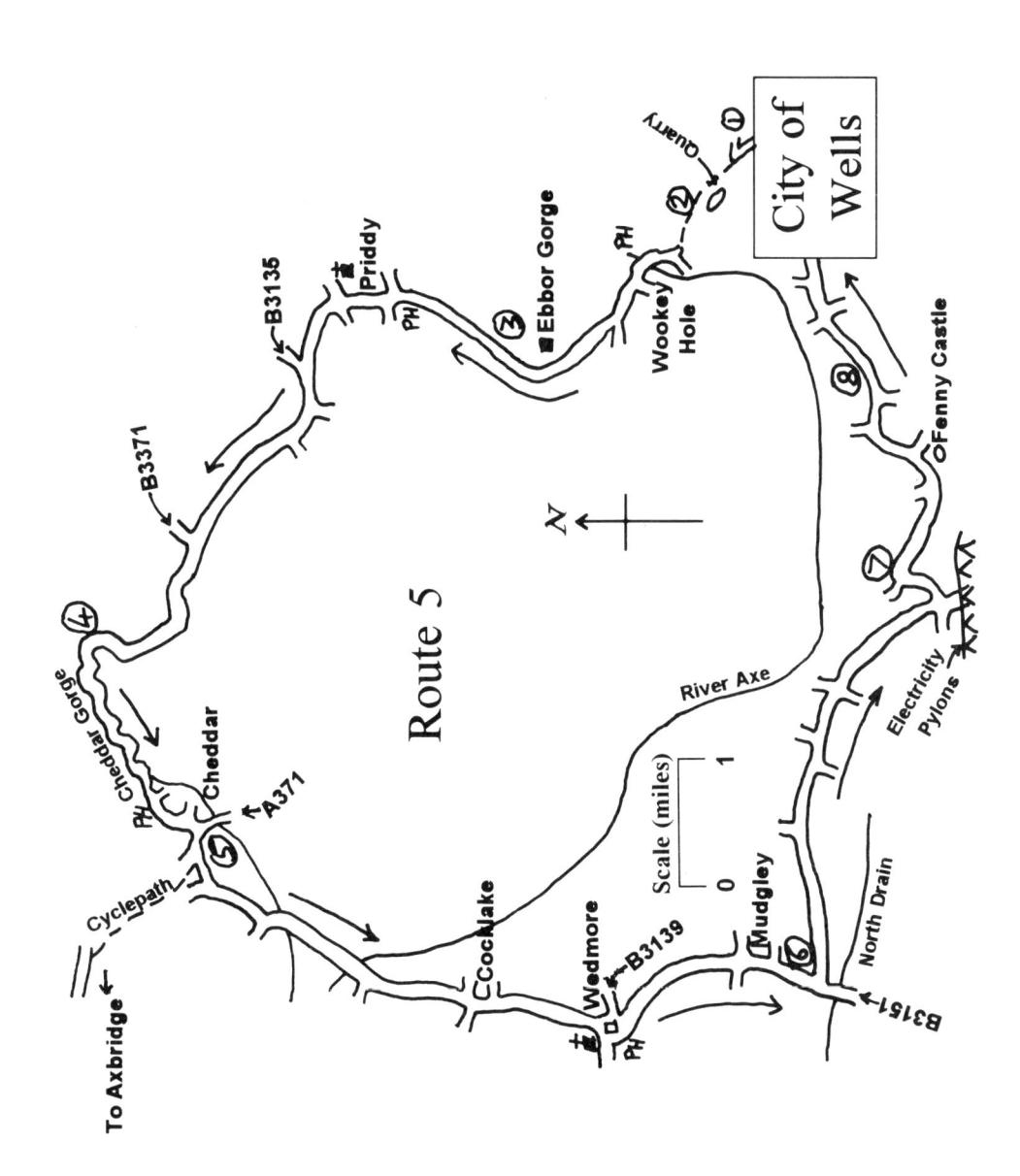

6. Once you are on the B3151, you will come to Wedmore in about 3 ½ miles. From here, you could cycle along the B3139 road all the way back to Wells. However, our route uses the much less busy and more scenic roads through the Somerset Levels. At the centre of Wedmore take the B3151 to Glastonbury. Pedal through Mudgley and about ½ a mile later turn left (if you've crossed over a wide canal-like river you have gone too far).

7. Now continue along this mostly straight road for about 5 miles, until you see some electricity pylons ahead of you. About 100 metres **before** you reach them, turn left at a crossroads and follow the sign to Wells.

8. You should soon arrive back at the city centre.

Outline to Route 6

Wells - East Horrington - Binegar - Stratton on the Fosse - Holcombe - Shepton Mallet - Wells

Distance: 24 miles

Grade: Strenuous

Map: O.S. 1:50,000 Landranger 183

Summary: This ride takes you to the East Mendips and towards the area most heavily used for quarrying. This end of the Mendips has much to offer which is frequently overlooked by people driving through. Give the ride a try.

You should not come across any quarry trucks on this route as it mostly steers clear of their dust-choked delivery roads. It is easy to ascertain which roads are used by the quarry lorries due to the dust which covers everything, including the trees and hedgerows. Millions of tonnes of limestone are blasted, crushed and transported from the area every year. A great deal of it goes to build new roads. Over the years this has scarred the landscape.

The route starts with a climb up into the Mendip Hills through East Horrington and onwards to Binegar. This stiff yet gradual pedal is not too bad. Further along at Stratton-on-the-Fosse you will see the magnificent Downside Abbey. This is now a Catholic Boys School. It is very much a part of the local community, bringing art and musical events to this remote area.

Now you can enjoy the mainly downhill stretch which eventually brings you to Shepton Mallet. You will free-wheel under the railway viaduct of the old Somerset and

Dorset line on the way into the town. This stretch of line was built in 1855. To some the S & D was known as the "Slow and Dirty"! The town rapidly grew up around the wool trade but experienced a crash at the start of the 19th century. Luckily the town had a secondary industry to fall back upon, that of drinks manufacture. Shepton Mallet is famed for the Showerings drink factory and more particularly "Babycham". The family firm started by selling beer and cider in the middle of the 19th century but it was not until 1953 that the pear drink was developed, using the famed Bambi Deer as promotion. More recently, the huge blue deer on top of the factory has gone due to changed circumstances and a new image, but the company is still in production. Shepton Mallet town centre is a nice place to wander around. The Market Cross has an interesting signpost on it which may be useful if you are thinking of a long distance cycle ride. Have a look, you will see what I mean.

The start of the ride back to Wells is very pleasant. The roads are narrow and little used by cars. There are some nice views to your left towards the Somerset Levels. Eventually you will come out onto the main road at Dulcote. The fountain is quite a feature here, and looks especially magical after a few days of frost. The ride back to Wells on the A371 is not very cycle-friendly but there is little alternative. It is about time that the disused railway line between Wells and Shepton Mallet was converted to a cycle path to make cycling safer and more attractive.

Route 6

1. The route starts from the Tourist Information Centre in Wells. Using the map on page 7, leave Wells on the Shepton Mallet Road. After a little way, fork left onto the B3139. This is St Thomas Street. Continue on this road for about ½ a mile.

2. A little way after the Britannia Inn turn right, following the road for East Horrington. Now you will have to do some serious pedalling up the hill through Horrington. When the road has flattened out somewhat take a left turn by Station House, following the signs to Cheddar and Priddy.

3. In about ½ a mile go straight at the B3135 and you will soon come to Binegar. At the first T-junction go left, and at the next, go right. This will bring you to the busy A37. Go right here and then immediately left, and then left

again all the time following the signs to Stratton-on-the-Fosse (about 2 ½ miles away).

4. You will eventually come out at the A367. You can get some nice views of Downside Abbey in this village. Go left along the main road and, after a few chicanes, turn right.

5. At the centre of Holcombe turn right for Stoke St Michael. About a mile further along take a right turn signposted Nettlebridge 1¼. Now look out for the left turn ahead, signposted Doulting 3½. Keep following the signs to Doulting until you come to a crossroads by the Wagon and Horses Inn.

6. Go straight ahead here and at a second crossroads, right. There is now a nice bit of downhill that takes you towards Shepton Mallet. As you approach the outskirts of the town, go straight ahead over the A37 and then left down the B3136. You arrive into Shepton Mallet down a hill, passing under an old railway viaduct on the way.

7. The town centre is a little confusing but essentially, go straight at the first roundabout and then right at the second. After about ½ a mile take a right turn signposted Wells 5.

8. Don't miss the next left turn signposted North Wootton 2. Continue down this pleasant stretch of road for a short while before taking an extremely sharp right turn, signed Wells 2 ½. You will come out at a T-junction near the A371. Go right and then left by the fountain.

9. Now pedal back to Wells along the main road until you see the 30 m.p.h. speed limit sign. On your left here you will see a path that will quickly take you to the city centre. Push your bike through the metal barriers and pedal around the moat of the Bishop's Palace back to the Cathedral.

Route 6

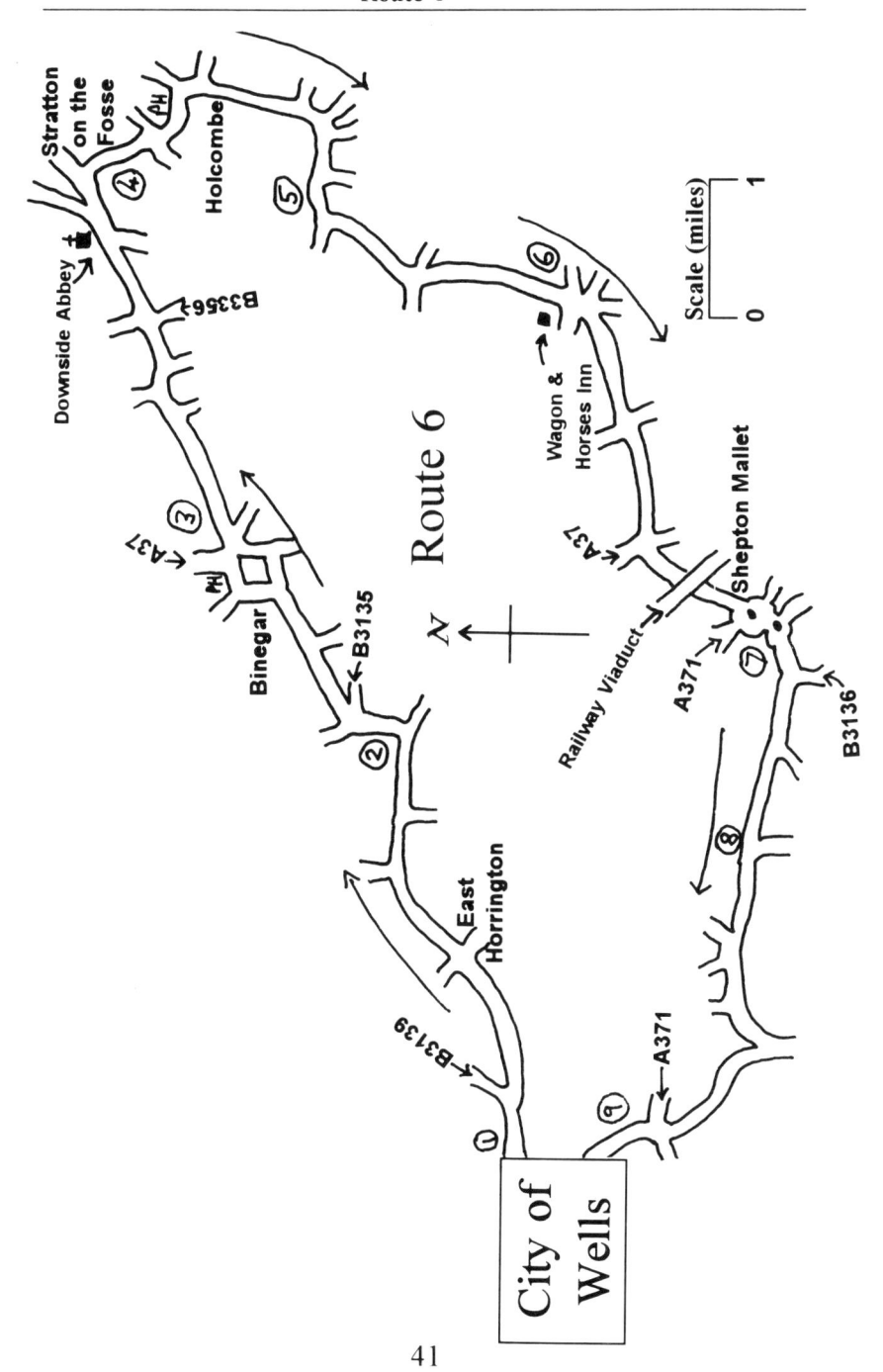

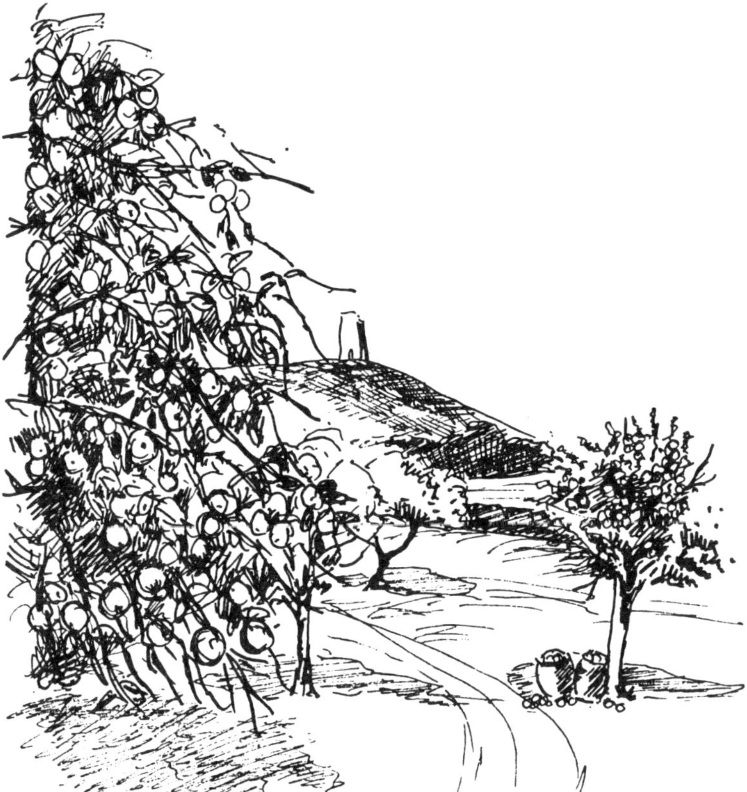

Outline to Route 7

Wells - Dulcote - North Wootton - Pilton - East Pennard - West Bradley - Baltonsborough - Glastonbury - Godney - Wells

Distance: 27 miles

Grade: Moderate

Map: O.S. 1:50,000 Landranger 182

Summary: If you are only on a short cycling trip to the area and you want to see as much variety as possible then this is the ride for you. In the space of a few miles you can visit the famous sites in Wells and Glastonbury, get a taste of the Somerset Levels and ride along some beautifully peaceful country lanes.

Starting from Wells you will very soon be in some wonderful countryside on the way to North Wootton. You can savour your last view of Glastonbury Tor for some time, on your right. From North Wootton it is not far to Pilton. This village has become well known as the venue for the annual Glastonbury Festival held during the summer, on nearby land at Worthy Farm. Over the years it has become a huge event with many famous names coming to perform on the stages. You will be able to see where the site is by the often gaily painted iron posts blocking gateways to the site.

Leaving Pilton, the route crosses a small ford which can make exhilarating cycling if water levels are high, and then passes over a disused railway line. The often deserted roads in this area can be a riot of colour in the spring and early summer. You can see Stitchwort and Wood Anemone flowers in the hedgerow as well as smelling Wild Garlic. The Cow Parsley can sometimes be so thick that it brushes against your arms as you cycle along. At the sides of the roads and more especially in the woods you may be able to see the wonderful sight of carpets of Bluebells.

The route now goes through a string of villages on the way to Glastonbury. This slightly raised area seems to be popular for growing fruit trees, with acres of them at every corner. Some of the farms advertise apples and cider for sale. Up until the turn of the century most farms would have made their own cider. Indeed many had special cider houses built with extra insulation to maintain the correct temperature for brewing. The process of manufacture is quite simple - in theory. The apples are first blended and then crushed to form what is known as pommance. This is then formed into a "Cheese". This is a carefully constructed mass of crushed apple and straw which is slowly pressed over many hours. The resulting juice is then fermented in barrels and should be ready to drink after a few months. It can be a deceivingly strong drink which may have a bad effect on your cycling!

The ride finishes off by visiting Glastonbury on the way back to Wells. There is plenty to see. For the location of The Tourist Information Office have a look at the map on page 7. For some nice views you can walk up the Tor. *Lock up your bicycle securely at the foot of the Tor.* The Abbey ruins are worth a visit if you have time. They are open all year round, 9.00am-6.00pm every day. There are quite a few nice cafes to have tea in and some alternative shops selling a variety of items such as crystals, herbs and aromatherapy oils.

From Glastonbury, the route back to Wells is one of my favourite. You will be pedalling along narrow roads through the Somerset levels. After Godney it is only a short distance back to Wells.

Route 7

1. You can start this ride from Wells or Glastonbury. If you want to start from Glastonbury turn to section 7 of this route guide, on page 47.

   Starting from Wells make your way to the Tourist Information Centre. From there, go under the arch to the Bishop's Palace and cycle along the moat to the right. At the end of this lane turn left, and continue to follow the moat. At the end of the road you will come to an iron barrier and the A371. (Unfortunately this busy road is the only route out of the city to the South-East). Go right and follow the road for about a mile until you reach Dulcote. Turn right in front of a fountain (*be careful of fast oncoming traffic*), pass under a railway arch and go immediately left.

2. At the next T-junction go left. You will soon arrive at Launcherley. Now go left at another crossroads and follow the signs all the way to Pilton, going through North Wootton en route.

3. You will come out on the A361 at Pilton. Take the one way street, straight ahead. After a few twists and turns you will find yourself in Bread Street. At the Long House Hotel turn right into Pylle Road.

4. Now take the next road on the right, signposted for East Pennard 2 miles. This is a very quiet stretch of road. Shortly, you should come to a ford, and a little further along, an intriguing house which used to be a railway signal box.

5. After quite a steep climb take a right turn signed for West Bradley. It is now a leisurely pedal for about a mile before a steep descent. At the next T-junction go right by a thatched cottage and follow the road through West

Short Cycle Rides Around Wells & Glastonbury

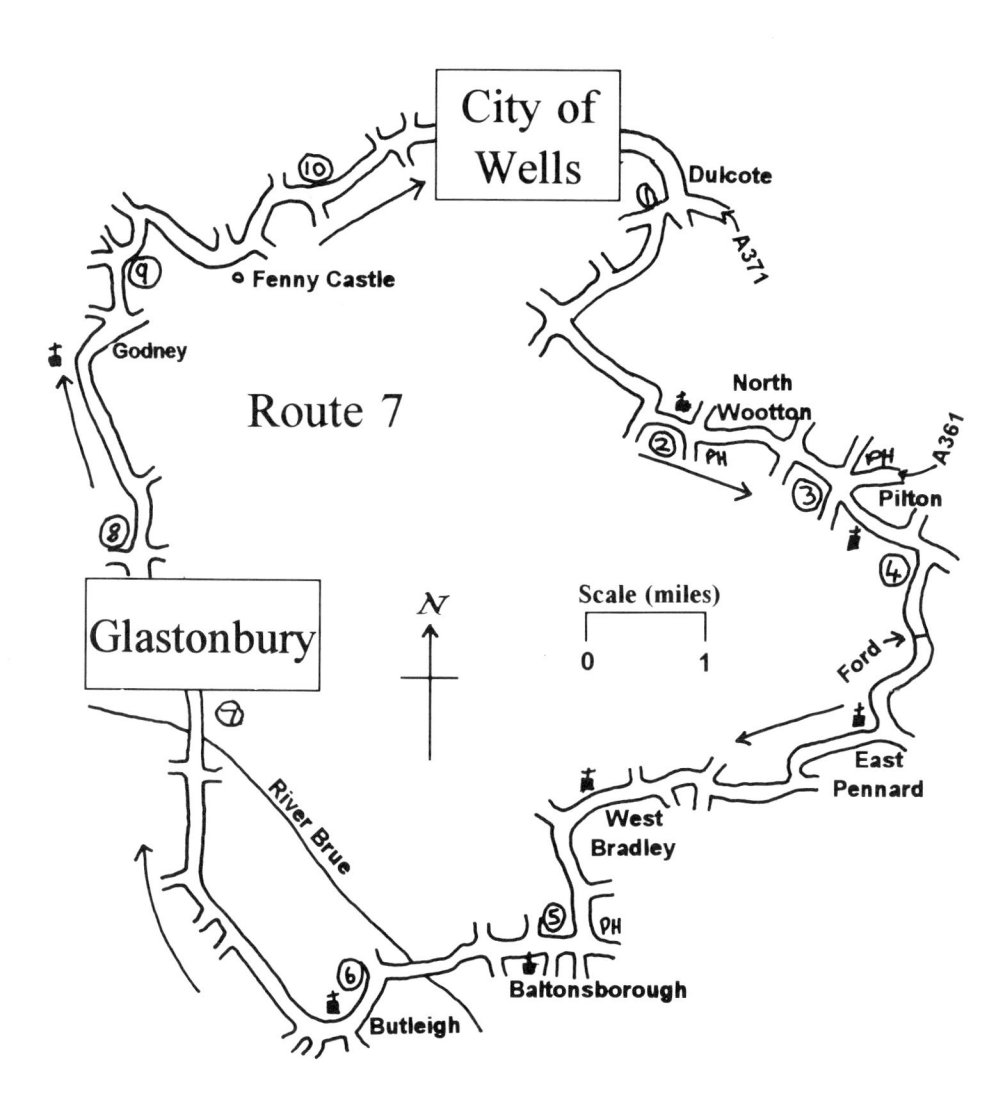

Route 7

Bradley. At the end of this village don't miss the left turn signed for Baltonsborough.

6. After going right at the next T-junction you will soon arrive at the Old Greyhound Pub at the centre of Baltonsborough. Go straight here. From about 1 mile after the village take the next 4 right turns, all the time following the signs for Glastonbury.

7. As you enter the outskirts of Glastonbury you will go up a steep hill to a main road. Go left and you will come to the town centre and the Abbey ruins via a mini roundabout. A look at the map on page 7 may help if you get lost.

8. Leaving Glastonbury, take the second exit on the left at the next roundabout (the B3151 road). This is signposted to Wedmore and Meare. Shortly, take the next road on the right following the sign to Godney.

9. At Godney go straight ahead at the first crossroads you come to, by a row of cottages adjacent to the river. Ignore the signpost which tells you to go right for Wells here, and pedal on to a second crossroads, where you turn right.

10. Now follow the signs all the way back to Wells along a quiet road which brings you directly into the city centre.

Outline to Route 8

Glastonbury - Coxbridge - West Bradley - Wraxall - Ditcheat - Castle Cary - East Lydford - Baltonsborough - Glastonbury

Distance: 29 miles

Grade: Moderate

Map: O.S. 1:50,000 Landranger 183

Summary: This rides makes a very pleasant day out. It will take you to the towns and villages East of Glastonbury. If you wish to visit the area by train, Castle Cary is the nearest British Rail Station. You could use this ride to get yourself to Glastonbury or Wells for some longer cycling trips.

As with several other routes in this book, you will start this ride with a pedal across Kennard Moor. This means getting yourself well off the beaten track almost as soon as you leave Glastonbury. The road follows alongside the River Brue for while. Fishing seems very popular here. I am told that there are also large numbers of eels in the rhynes and rivers. Nearer the coast there is a huge annual spring harvests of elvers or baby eels. Incredibly, they start life in the Sargasso Sea 4,000 miles away. They slowly make their way to the mouths of rivers like the Parrett or the Brue and swarm up them in their thousands. Once caught, they are sent all over Britain and the world, sometimes by aeroplane to keep them fresh. Those that remain, seep into all the water channels on the moors. It can be creepy to think that there are hundreds of eels all around you as you cycle along,

Lock-up, Castle Cary

but thankfully most of them stay well out of site.

The ride continues on from the moors to a string of villages on the higher ground to the East of Glastonbury - first West Bradley, then Wraxall and Ditcheat. The village name of Wraxall also occurs in the Cotswolds. It refers to Buzzards or Crows once being common on nearby land. The church at Ditcheat is a magnificent building. Have a look round, if you have time.

Castle Cary is a nice place to stop on this ride. Don't expect there to be a castle to view now. The Norman castle built by the Lovel Family was abandoned 800 years ago and none of it remains today. It is said that the stone from the castle has gone to build the houses in the town. Castle Cary has a relaxed feel to it and can be enjoyable to wander around. The small Market House Museum in the central square is open during the summer, Mon.-Fri. 10.00am-12.30pm and 2.30pm-4.30pm. Have a look out for the town lock-up in Castle Square. It was built during the 1780's and is very similar to others in this area.

From Castle Cary it seems quite a long way through very isolated countryside to the next village of East Lydford, then it is back onto the Somerset Levels again. If you are cycling on the Levels for the first time, and it is summer, sooner or later you will notice the huge numbers of Dragonflies and Damselflies. Although they have fearsome nicknames like "Horse Stingers" and "Devil's Darning Needles" they are harmless and sometimes quite inquisitive. On some days, if a particular species has recently emerged, there can be so many that it is difficult not to run them over. Up to 25 different species have been identified on the Levels, some of them extremely rare. On hot summer days it can be relaxing to picnic by a river and watch the Damselflies flitting along the banks. However, you are more likely to see Dragonflies further from water. The larger species sometimes hunt by hawking along a beat, then suddenly darting off in pursuit of a passing insect.

Route 8

1. This route starts from the centre of Glastonbury. Use the map on page 7 to find your way to the start of the ride.
2. Having turned into Cinnamon Lane, freewheel down the hill and take the next road on the right. Now follow this long, narrow lane until you come to a T-junction. Turn left here, then right, and then right again taking the West Bradley road.
3. Cycle through West Bradley and continue on this road

Route 8

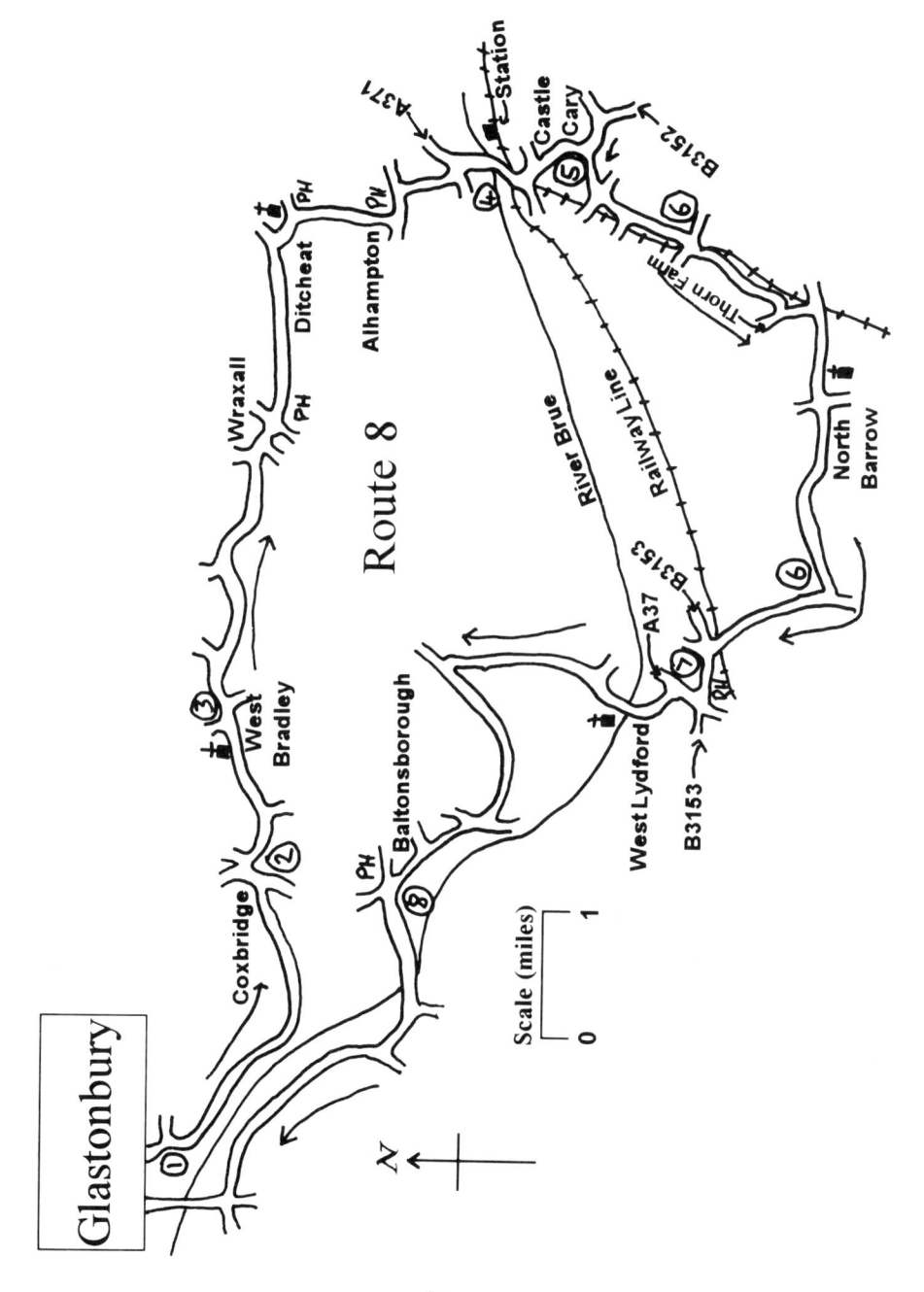

following the signs to Ditcheat.

4. Now follow the road signs to Castle Cary. In a while you will join the A371. Turn right and pedal past Castle Cary Railway Station and cross over the bridge beyond. If you do not want to cycle along this road there is a footpath for you to push your bicycle along. In a short while turn right, following the sign to Castle Cary.

5. After going up and then down a short hill follow the sign to the town centre, on your left. Remember where you are because you will have to return by this road.
To leave Castle Cary, return to Station Road, and pedal back the way you came, but after about 100 metres turn left into Torbay Road. This is the road for North Barrow.

6. There seem few signposts around here but if you follow this road, you will first cross over the railway line opposite a turning to Cockhill, and then arrive at a T-junction (beyond the one to Higher Thorn Farm). Turn right and continue on to a crossroads beyond North Barrow. Go straight ahead here and onwards to another T-junction. Turn right and head for the Lydfords.

7. At the B3153 road turn left. You will soon come to the busy A37 by the Cross Keys Inn. Turn right and pedal along the main road for a short while (there is a footpath along here) before turning left for West Lydford. Pass the Church and take the next left turn. This is **not** signposted. In about 2 miles take another left turn, this time signposted, Baltonsborough 2 ½ miles.

8. You will soon arrive at the Old Greyhound Inn at the centre of Baltonsborough. Turn left here and pedal back onto the Somerset Levels. From about 1 mile after the village take the next 4 right turns, all the time following the signs for Glastonbury. As you enter the town you will go up a steep hill to a T-junction. Go left and you will come to the town centre.

Outline to Route 9

Glastonbury - Street - Charlton Mackrell - Somerton - Pitney - Langport - High Ham - Ashcott - Glastonbury

Distance: 30 miles (optional 2 miles off road)

Grade: Moderate

Maps: O.S. 1:50,000 Landranger 182, 183, 193

Summary: Leave plenty of time to do this ride. Not because it is long, it isn't, but because there is so much to see. You will visit attractive towns such as Langport and Somerton, go through very varied countryside and there is also some off road cycling for mountain bike enthusiasts.

The ride starts with a pedal to Street, a town built up around the shoe-making trade. Why not stop and have a look around the shoe museum on the way through. It is open during the summer every day except Sunday, and entrance is free.

As you pedal away from Street, up the hill, you can see the monument to Sir Samuel Hood on your right. There is an inscription around the base which may be of interest to naval historians. After the climb there is a long stretch of steady freewheeling which brings you to Charlton Mackrell.

From here to Somerton and Langport there are some good "off road" tracks to cycle along if you wish. Somerton makes a nice place to stop and wander around. The county of Somerset is supposed to have been named after this town. The name means "sea lake enclosure". In about 450 AD, due to climatic changes, the water levels rose in this area, making it necessary for the villagers to move to higher ground. Thus Somerton was founded, and grew to become the capital of Wessex. It can be relaxing to sit down in the square (recovering from the push up the hill) and watch the world go by. You could stop in one of the pubs or tea-shops. Don't over-indulge though, you still have plenty of pedalling to do.

Huish Episcopi and Langport are not far away. You can't miss the magnificent tower of St Mary's Church as you come into the town. Near here, the thatched 17th century Rose and Crown Inn looks inviting. A little further along you will pass under the Hanging Chapel built in 1354. This was part of the ancient city wall. Langport itself, as the name implies, used to be a busy port, mainly during Roman times. However, the river had silted up and become largely disused by the time of the Norman conquest. The buildings at the bottom end of town, near the river, are renowned for suffering from structural problems. This is because their fronts were built on the sturdy Roman causeway and their backs on the soft river mud. Have a look; you will see what I mean.

The route now continues on quiet roads to High Ham. The church here has some comical stone carvings around the outside. If you don't fancy stopping for refreshments at the pub in the village you will soon be freewheeling down to King's Sedge Moor and cycling across to Pedwell and Ashcott. These villages grew up because they were on the higher ground of the Polden Hills and did not suffer from the regular floods which affected the moors. From here it is only a short pedal through the peat fields back to Glastonbury.

Route 9

1. The route starts from the entrance to the Abbey ruins in the centre of Glastonbury. Using the map on page 7, follow the cycle route to Street. Don't forget that you want to go down Benedict Street from the first roundabout in Glastonbury.

2. As you enter Street, follow the signs for the High Street. After you have bumped over the third or forth "sleeping policeman" turn left into Vestry Road. Now go straight ahead at several crossroads until you come out at the B3151 road. Turn right and pedal up the hill to a crossroads where you go left.

3. Soon you will be gently freewheeling down a long hill. Follow the signs to Charlton Mackrell. As you are entering the village, you can choose which way you go.

    a. **For mountain bikers**, turn right into Summer Lane as you enter Charlton Mackrell. *This track is mostly easy pedalling but be very careful on the difficult, steep downhill section just before you come back to the road. You may want to get off and push here.* Once back on metalled road turn right then left onto the B3153, following the signs to Somerton.

    b. **For non-mountain bikers** pedal under the railway line at Charlton Mackrell, to a junction beyond. Now follow the signs to Somerton.

4. As you approach Somerton, don't miss the tricky right turn. *Be careful here.* Now pedal up the hill to a roundabout and turn left along North Street. From here you again have a choice.

    a. **For mountain bikers**, leave Somerton on the Langport road, but when you are almost out of the town, fork right into Bancombe Road (this could be signposted for the

South Somerset Cycle Route although the sign has currently been turned the wrong way). Take the second road on the left, signposted for Westcombe, and continue straight for about 2 miles. The track can be quite wet and muddy. Eventually you will return to metalled road at a crossroads. Go straight ahead here then take the second left turn. Now go through Pitney and onto the B3151 beyond, where you go right. Now take the second road on the left following the cycle route sign.

b. **For non-mountain bikers,** follow the B3153 road to Langport. After about 3 miles look out for two left turns at the bottom of a hill, one either side of a bridge over the river. Take the second of these turns. It is currently signed for the South Somerset Cycle Route.

5. After about a mile you will come out at the A372 road. Go right and pedal to a junction by St Mary's Church. Fork left here and continue uphill, under the Hanging Chapel, to the centre of Langport. Turn right at the main road (Cheapside).

6. The next section is quite tricky. Pedal out of town on the Somerton road until you come to a crossroads. Turn left, this is signposted to Wearne. You will soon come to a T-junction. Go right and then very shortly left, up a steep hill. Now look out for the next right turn. This will lead you down a very narrow road to a cottage. Pedal on up the hill beyond and you will come out at a T-junction. The route becomes easier to follow now. If you turn left you will first go through High Ham, and then onwards to Pedwell.

7. At the A361 go right then immediately left up Pedwell Hill. In about 100 metres go right into Pedwell Lane. You will come out at the busy A39. *Take great care here.* Go straight ahead up the hill opposite, into Ashcott.

Route 9

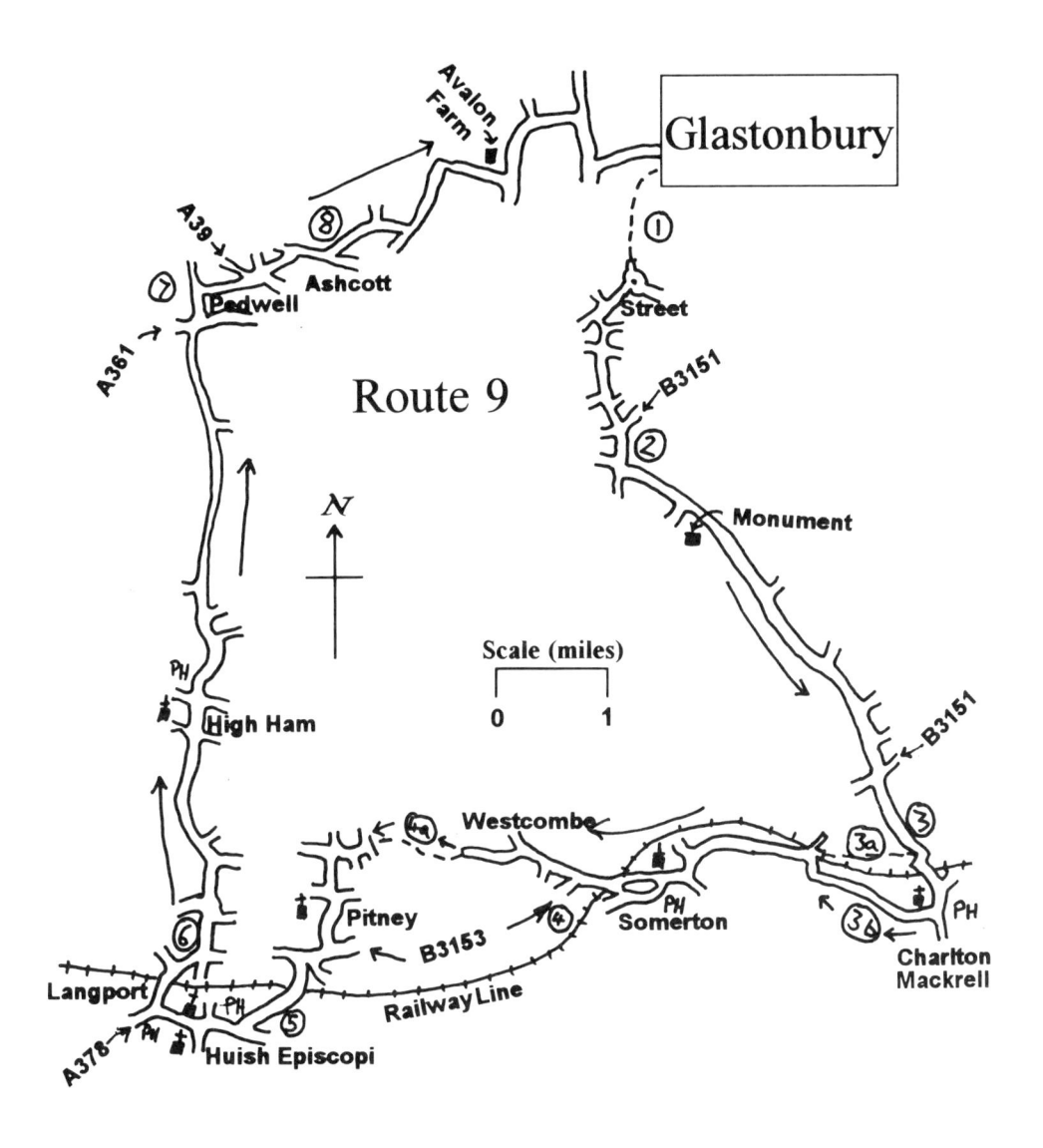

At a T-junction go right and continue past the village hall and church to another a T-junction with Whitley Road. Turn right and freewheel down the hill out of the village.

8. On the way down the hill take the first left turn. It is not signposted so don't miss this one. After about 2 miles you will come out at another T-junction by Avalon Farm. Go left here and pedal on until you come to yet another T-junction. Turn right then, after about ¼ of a mile, left. If you follow this road you will arrive back at the centre of Glastonbury.

Hanging Chapel, Langport

Outline to Route 10

Wells - Wookey Hole - Priddy - Blagdon - Ubley - Chew Stoke - Bishop Sutton - East Harptree - Wells

Distance: 32 miles or 21 miles

Grade: Strenuous

Map: O.S. 1:50,000 Landranger 182

Summary: This cycle ride is all about contrast. Cycling up and over the Mendip Hills to the Chew Valley beyond is an experience not to be missed. I found it quite hard work but it makes a fantastic day out. You can always take the shorter route if you do not feel up to a 32 mile pedal. You will still be able to see the lakes and rolling countryside from the northern ridge of the Mendips.

There is no doubt that it is hard work pedalling up to Priddy at the start of this ride. Take it slowly - I push up many of the hills. On the way up, the view behind you is superb. You may even be able to see the sea to your right. Priddy village is well spread out along the road and has a good mixture of old and newer properties. Although it is very much an agricultural centre today, it was once a lead mining village. There is evidence that the Romans mined lead in this area of the Mendips, but the industry reached its peak during the mid 17th century. Mining activity lasted a long time. The St Cuthberts lead works near Priddy only closed down in 1908. Some areas of land in the Mendips are not grazed by livestock because of the effects of lead poisoning. Today, the houses have water piped to them, as with anywhere else, but many years ago the miners were known for going mad and dying at an early age. Even today local

The Green, Priddy

farmers know better than to plough too deep lest they disturb the lead in the soil.

Beyond Priddy the Mendips become very baron, harsh and treeless. It can often be windy here, and several degrees colder than when you set off from Wells. A few miles further along, as you pedal through a very bleak area, it is refreshing to see Charterhouse Church in the distance. It was built in 1908 and looks as if it should be in a small settlement on a Scottish Island.

In another mile or so you will come to the escarpment that leads you down to Chew Valley and the famous lakes. Blagdon Lake, in front of you, was created in 1901 whereas the larger Chew Valley Lake was opened by Queen Elizabeth 1 in 1956. Both lakes are very popular for fishing and bird-watching. Also Chew Valley Lake has an active sailing club. These reservoirs are important sources of water for Bristol.

You will now have pedalled into the neighbouring County of Avon. The villages here, such as Blagdon and Ubley, still have the Mendip charm even though this area is firmly within the Bristol commuter belt. Away from the lakes the countryside has a rough wildness. Look out for the signposts which have been used for target practice. I only thought that happened in the wild west!

Once around the Chew Valley Lake you will have to prepare yourself for the climb back onto the Mendips. On the way, East Harptree is a pleasant village. I am told that the word Harptree means "the military road by the wood" in Old English. By the look of the clock opposite the T-junction in the centre of the village, they obviously thought a lot of Queen Victoria. If you are feeling thirsty or tired as you pedal back to Wells, there are 2 lonely Inns to visit. Firstly there is the Castle of Comfort, and shortly after, the Hunters Lodge.

Route 10

1. Starting from the centre of Wells, use the directions in Route 5 to get to Priddy.
2. From the centre of Priddy, cycle up the hill past the tiny Post Office to the crossroads with the B3135 road. Go straight ahead and in about 2 miles, go straight ahead again at the junction with the B3371 and pedal on to a T-junction.
3. **Long Route** You should now be at the B3134 road. Turn left, following the signs for Burrington. In about ½ a mile fork right along Two Trees, and freewheel down the hill to Blagdon. *Be extremely careful coming down this hill especially in wet conditions. It is very steep.* Now continue the route guide from section 4.

   Short Route At the T-junction with the B3134 road turn right. Now take the next left turn signposted West Harptree 3. Keep going straight at 2 crossroads until you come to a third, opposite Mead Cottage, above East Harptree Village. *This last section of road can be very muddy, making it slippery in wet weather.* Go right here and start to pedal up a long steep hill. Now continue the route guide from section 7.
4. At the end of the road turn right onto the A368 by the Seymour Arms. I do not usually include sections of "A" roads in my routes but in this case the traffic is generally not too bad. After about 2 miles take the first turning on the left. Although this is not signposted it will lead you to Ubley. At the far end of the village turn left down Snatch Lane, by the war memorial.
5. Now follow the signs to Chew Stoke which is about 5 miles away. You will pass alongside Chew Valley Lake on the way. As you are entering Chew Stoke you will

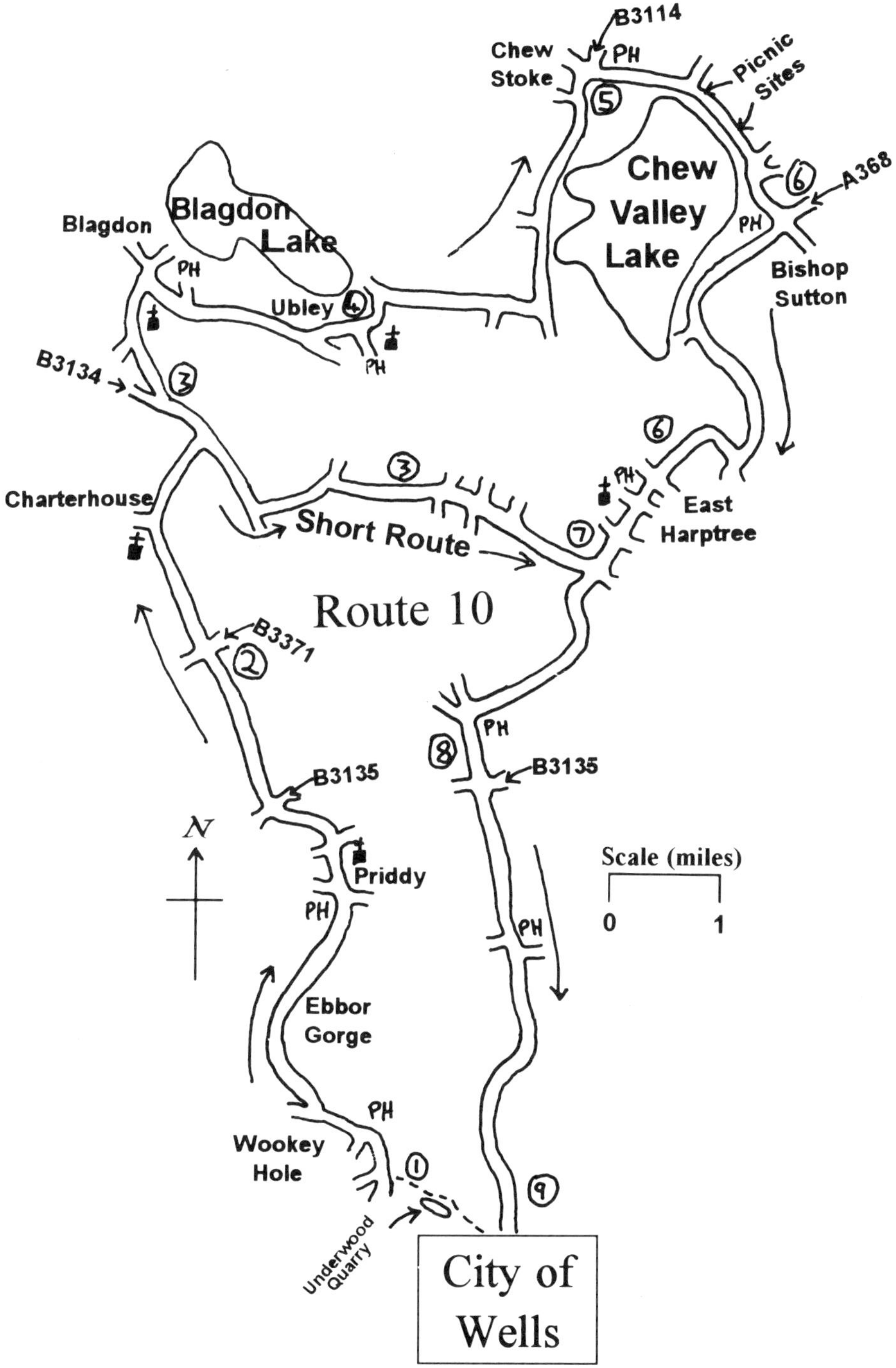
B3114
Chew Stoke
PH
Picnic Sites
5
Chew Valley Lake
6
A368
PH
Bishop Sutton
Blagdon
Blagdon Lake
PH
Ubley
4
PH
B3134
3
6
3
PH
Charterhouse
East Harptree
Short Route
7
Route 10
B3371
2
8
PH
B3135
B3135
N
Priddy
Scale (miles)
0
1
PH
PH
Ebbor Gorge
PH
Wookey Hole
1
9
Underwood Quarry
City of Wells

come down quite a steep hill. Don't go too fast because just beyond the Stoke Inn you must turn right, into Wallycourt Road. You will soon be pedalling beside the lake again. If you want to stop, there are 2 picnic sites on your right along this stretch. The first one has the Chew Valley Lake Information Centre, a café and toilets but the second would be better if you wanted a quiet picnic.

6. At the end of this long section of road turn right, following the signs for Bishop Sutton. When you come to the A368 Road go right and pedal through Bishop Sutton village and on for another ½ mile. Now take the left turn signposted for East Harptree and when you come to the crossroads with the B3114, go straight ahead up East Harptree High Street. At the T-junction by the village shop go left, and then immediately right.

7. You now have the strenuous task of pedalling (and probably pushing) up the hill to the top of the Mendips. Take it slowly, looking behind you as you go. You will get some fine views of the lakes.

8. Keep going straight ahead until the road flattens out, and you arrive at the Castle of Comfort Inn. Turn left here and you will firstly pass along the top of the Mendips and then freewheel down the hill into Wells. *Do not get carried away with the speed going down this hill, especially in wet or icy conditions. Also, at the time of writing, the road surface is rather uneven.*

9. At the bottom of the hill turn left, then immediately right, and you will quickly find yourself back in the city centre.

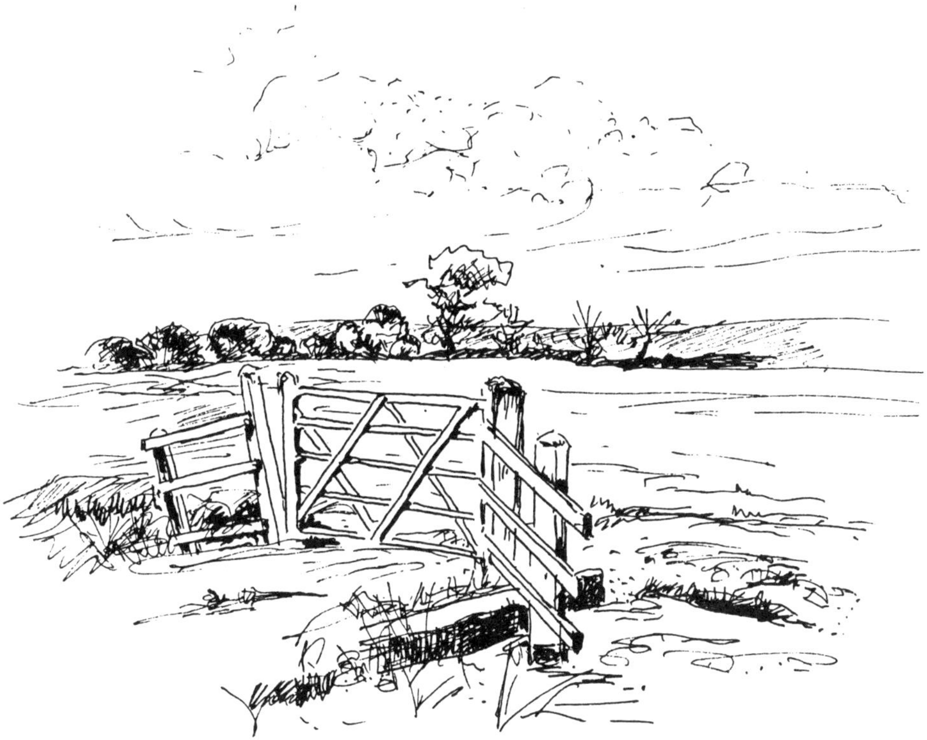

Index

Acetyl-salicylic Acid 32
Apple Blossom 22
Apples 17
Ashcott 53
Aspirin 32
Avalon Farm 30
Axbridge 32,34
Babysham 38
Baltonsborough 16,43,48
Barton St David 16
Binegar 37
Bishop Sutton 59
Bishop's Palace, Wells 45
Bittersharps, apples 22
Bittersweets, apples 22
Blagdon 59
Blagdon Lake 61
Bleadney 11
Bluebells 44
Britannia Inn 39
Bulrushes 28
Burrington 62
Burtle 27
Butleigh 16
Buzzard 18
Castle Cary 48
Castle Cary BR Station 48,52
Castle of Comfort Inn 61
Catcott 27
Chalice Well 16
Charlton Mackrell 53
Charterhouse 61
Cheddar Gorge 32
Cheddar Reservoir 34
Cheddar Show Caves 32
Chew Stoke 59
Chew Valley Lake 61
Chew Valley Lake
 -Information Centre 64
Cider 17,22,44
Cider Cheese 44

Cider Making 44
Cider Truck 17
Cinnamon Lane 50
Clarks Shoe Factory 18
Cloisters Café 44
Cockhill 52
Compton Dundon 16
Cotton Grass 27
Cow Parsley 44
Coxbridge 21,48
Coxley 21
Damselfly 50
Devil's Darning Needle 50
Ditcheat 48
Downside Abbey 37
Dragonfly 50
Dulcote 38,43
East Harptree 59,61
East Horrington 37
East Lydford 48
East Mendip 37
East Pennard 43
Easton 11
Ebbor Gorge 11,31
Elvers 48
Fenny Castle 11,23
Ford 12,14,43
Glastonbury Abbey 44
Glastonbury Festival 43
Glastonbury Tor 24,44
Godney 21,27,43
Grey Heron 21
Hanging Chapel 54
Higher Thorn Farm 52
High Ham 53
Hodgkinson 12
Holcombe 37
Horse Stingers 50
Huish Episcopi 54
Hunters Lodge Inn 61
Jacobs Ladder 32

Kennard Moor 16,21,48
Kestrel 18
King Cups 22
King's Sedge Moor 54
Langport 53
Launcherley 45
Lead Mines 59
Lead Poisoning 59
Lockup Castle Cary 50
Lovel Family 49
Market House Museum 50
Marsh Marigold 22
Mendip Hills 11,59
Mudgley 31
North Barrow 52
North Wootton 43
Old Greyhound Inn 47,52
Pavey's Lookout Tower 32
Peat Moors Visitor Centre 28
Peat workings 27
Pedwell 54
Pilton 43
Pine Tree Farm 24
Pitney 53
Polden Hills 28,54
Pollarding 32
Priddy 31,59
Priddy Fair 22,31
Queen's Sedge Moor 21
Red Lion Inn, W Pennard 24
Redlake farm 24
Reedmace 27
Rhynes 21,48
River Axe 12
River Brue 30,48
River Parrett 48
Rose & Crown Inn 54
Rose & Portcullis Inn 20
Rural Life Museum 16
Sir Samuel Hood 18,53
Sargasso Sea 48
Shapwick 27
Sharps, apples 22

Shepton Mallet 37
Shoe Museum 18,53
Showerings 38
Somerset & Dorset Railway 37,38
Somerton 53
Sphagnum Moss 27
St Cuthbert's lead Mines 59
St Thomas St. Wells 39
St. Mary's Church 54
Stitchwort 43
Stoke Inn 64
Stone Quarrying 37
Stratton-on-the-Fosse 37
Street 16,53
Sweet Track 28
Sweets, apples 22
Ubley 59
Underwood Quarry 31
Wagon & Horses Inn 40
Wearne 56
Wedmore 31
Wessex 54
West Bradley 43, 48
West Pennard 21
Westhay 27
Wild Garlic 44
Willow 32
Wocig 12
Wood Anemone 43
Wookey Hole 11,31,59
Worthy farm, Pilton 43
Wraxall 48,49
Yellow Flag Iris 22

Cycleway Books

As well as this publication, Cycleway Books have already brought out the extremely successful

Short Cycle Rides Around Bath

This book, also by John Plaxton, contains 12 cycle routes which take you along the canals, cyclepaths and country lanes around the Georgian City. It has now been reprinted due to popular demand and is available from bookshops and cycleshops, or direct from the publishers.

If you have difficulty in obtaining copies of any of our publications, write to us at

**Cycleway Books
2 Cork Terrace
Bath BA1 3BE**

Please state how many copies of the books you require, making cheques payable to **John Plaxton**.

Each book is £3.95. Postage and packaging are free.